# ACKNOWLEDGMENTS

Behind *Who Believes What?* lies the work of many individuals who made the final design and graphics for this book possible.

A huge thank-you goes to all our experts for their invaluable assistance as we worked together, discussing each individual scene and subject, correcting the tiniest details of the text and illustrations for accuracy. Without their support, this book would not have been possible. We would especially like to thank Kristina Dohrn, Dr. Britta Frede, Michael Gerhard, Volker Knirsch, Dr. Gabriele Richter, Dr. Markus Thurau, Daniel Vorpahl, and Jenny Vorpahl.

Owlkids Books would like to thank David Belfon, Dr. Simon Appolloni, Dr. Lara Braitstein, and Hassam Munir for their review of the English language edition of the book.

Text and illustrations © 2017 Beltz & Gelberg
in the publishing group Beltz – Weinheim Basel
Translated and adapted by Shelley Tanaka

Published in English in 2018 by Owlkids Books Inc.
Published in German under the title *Das Wimmelbuch der Weltreligionen* in 2017

Owlkids Books acknowledges the financial support of the Canada Council for the Arts, the Ontario Arts Council, the Government of Canada through the Canada Book Fund (CBF) and the Government of Ontario through the Ontario Creates Book Initiative for our publishing activities.

Owlkids Books gratefully acknowledges that our office in Toronto is located on the traditional territory of many nations, including the Mississaugas of the Credit, the Chippewa, the Wendat, the Anishinaabeg, and the Haudenosaunee Peoples.

Published in Canada by Owlkids Books Inc.,
1 Eglinton Avenue East, Toronto, ON M4P 3A1

Published in the US by Owlkids Books Inc.,
1700 Fourth Street, Berkeley, CA 94710

Library and Archives Canada Cataloguing in Publication

Wills, Anna, 1978-
[Wimmelbuch der Weltreligion. English]
    Who believes what? : exploring the world's major religions /
Anna Wills, Nora Tomm ; translated by Shelley Tanaka.

Includes index.
Translation of: Das Wimmelbuch der Weltreligionen.
ISBN 978-1- 77147-333-0 (hardcover)

    1. Religions—Juvenile literature. I. Tomm, Nora, 1979–, illustrator
II. Tanaka, Shelley, translator  III. Title.  IV. Title: Wimmelbuch der Weltreligion.  English.

BL92.W5413 2018          j200          C2018-900295-6

Library of Congress Control Number: 2018930804

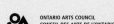

FSC MIX
Paper from responsible sources
FSC™ C004888
www.fsc.org

Manufactured in Chai Wan, Hong Kong, in April 2023, by Printing Express Ltd.
Job #2023-03-001

D    E    F    G    H    I

ONTARIO ARTS COUNCIL
CONSEIL DES ARTS DE L'ONTARIO
an Ontario government agency
un organisme du gouvernement de l'Ontario

Canada Council
for the Arts
Conseil des Arts
du Canada

Canada

Owlkids  Publisher of Chirp, Chickadee and OWL
www.owlkidsbooks.com

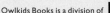

Owlkids Books is a division of  bayard canada

Anna Wills    Nora Tomm

# Who Believes What?

## Exploring the World's Major Religions

Translated by Shelley Tanaka

OWLKIDS BOOKS

# CONTENTS

# WHAT IS RELIGION?

**M**any people try, with the help of a religion, to find answers to life's big questions. What happens after death? How should we live? How will I live? What is right, and what is wrong? What is the meaning of life? Each religion offers its own path and its own answers.

The five major world religions—Hinduism, Judaism, Buddhism, Christianity, and Islam—are very old. And in addition to these five, there are many other faiths and denominations. Not everyone belongs to a religion. Some people leave their religion or move from one faith to another. Other people were not brought up in religious families and have never believed.

In some religions there is only one god. Others have several gods, or none at all. Some religions have a book where the rules and stories of that religion are written down. Others place more value on beliefs shared by word of mouth, called oral tradition. This can include storytelling and jokes, songs and dance, and other cultural customs passed from generation to generation.

Religion has a lot to do with community—celebrating with others, following rituals, practicing a common lifestyle, perhaps even dressing a certain way. Rituals and community provide everyday life with structure and give people support through difficult times. Religions also have rules about, for example, how you should behave toward other people or what you're allowed to eat. And many religions have beliefs in common, such as the belief that it is wrong to kill or to steal.

What you believe is a deeply personal decision. The freedom to choose whether to believe and what to believe is so important that it is even embedded in the Universal Declaration of Human Rights, one of the core documents of the United Nations. In many countries, freedom of religion is written into the highest levels of law, including the US Constitution and the Canadian Charter of Rights and Freedoms.

Religion is an important part of the lives of people of faith. It is also part of every culture and influences the lives of those who belong to no religion at all! So let's take some time to explore the beliefs and customs of people around the world. Knowing more about others helps us to better understand one another, find ideas we share, and live side by side in community.

## HINDUISM

Hinduism is the third-largest religion in the world. It originated in India and today is still mostly practiced in South Asia. Most Hindus are born into the religion, and people debate whether it is even possible to convert to it.

Hinduism is made up of various traditions that have overlapped and sometimes joined together. It has many different gods and goddesses, and they are worshipped in their own particular ways. Even today, new gods are being added. Some Hindus worship a singular divinity behind all of them.

 As a whole, Hinduism has no leader, no fixed set of teachings or laws, no central institution, and no single book. It relies on oral as much as written tradition.

Hindus are connected by a common way of life and a social order that can be divided into many units. The smallest unit is the extended family. The largest units are the four classes of society, called varnas. These can again be divided into a vast number of groups  called castes, or jati. Each person is born into a caste and can leave it only upon death. Each caste has its own principles and duties. There are rules governing everything, from meals to marriage. One must follow these rules to be considered pure, in both body and behavior.

Hindus believe that a new life begins after death. This is called reincarnation. They also believe that every living being, whether human, animal, or plant, has a soul. Your behavior in your previous life will determine which caste you're reborn into and whether you're reborn as an animal, a plant, or a human. This is called karma. For many Hindus, the goal is to eventually be free from the cycle of reincarnation. One way to achieve this is through self-denial and giving up earthly possessions. Other Hindus focus on developing a loving relationship with God.

In Hinduism, some forms of dance are considered a sacred act and a way to explain and pass down religious knowledge. ▶

There are many religious rules about cleanliness at meals. Banana leaves are considered clean, since new ones are used to serve each meal.

The philosopher Uddalaka Aruni believed that the human soul and nature's soul were one. He told his son to break open the seed of a fig, saying, "This tiny seed that you can barely see will grow into a huge tree. Believe in this tiny thing, my dear son. This is your very self, your soul. This is you!"

Three lotus petals fell from the hands of the creator god Brahma, and where they touched the earth arose the holy city of Pushkar.

The god Brahma is associated with creation.

Grihastha is the second of four stages of life, when a person finds a partner and raises a family.

◀ Ritushuddhi is a coming-of-age ritual marked by a girl's first menstruation.

B.R. Ambedkar was a lawyer and politician who fought for the rights of Dalits, who are at the bottom of the Hindu caste system.

A puja is a form of worship, usually with prayer and offerings. Here it honors the goddess Santoshi Mata.

◀ Upanayana is a rite of passage, when a boy belonging to one of the top three castes receives the sacred thread to wear across his chest.

Plants and animals are worshipped along with gods. Tulsi is an Indian basil associated with the god Vishnu.

The sitar is an Indian stringed instrument.

Navaratri is a festival that lasts for nine nights and honors the divine mother. ▶

At a wedding, the couple is connected by a thread, which represents their bond. As part of the wedding ceremony, the couple lights and circles a fire. Their first steps together symbolize the beginning of their marriage.

Metal is considered particularly pure. People who can afford to do so will eat from their own metal bowl.

Many Hindus prefer to eat meals cooked at home according to religious rules and transported to the workplace by a delivery service.

◀ A kolam is a drawing made with rice flour. It is said to bring good fortune.

Brahmacharya is the first stage of life, when a young person gains worldly and spiritual knowledge.

◀ Handprints are placed beside the entrance to protect the home.

Ghee is clarified butter made from cow's milk. It is used in both cooking and in rituals.

At a funeral, the eldest son lights the cremation fire. Afterward the ashes are scattered in the Ganges River.

Head shaving marks the beginning of several rituals. It is a sign that a person has turned away from all earthly things to devote herself to her faith.

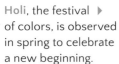

Holi, the festival ▶ of colors, is observed in spring to celebrate a new beginning.

Every act leaves its mark on the human soul. This is called karma. Bathing in the Ganges River is seen as cleansing the soul of impurities. ▶

Gods can take many forms. The Ganges River embodies the goddess Ganga, but it is also a holy river that can be worshipped with a puja.

# HINDUISM

**Sannyasa** is the fourth stage of life, when a person devotes all his energy to achieving freedom from reincarnation with intensive meditation.

**Diwali** is the festival of light. Observed in autumn, it celebrates the triumph of good over evil.

**Lakshmi** is the goddess of success and prosperity. She is the wife of the god Vishnu.

The god **Vishnu** protects and preserves the universe.

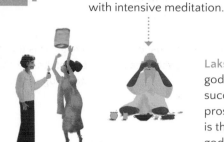

Places where a religious ceremony will be performed must be ritually cleansed.

Historically, **Dalits** are discriminated against for traditionally doing the dirtiest manual jobs, which exposes them to ritual impurity. B.R. Ambedkar proclaimed, "We, too, are human beings like others!"

Only women wear the **bindi** mark on their foreheads. Today the bindi mostly serves as a fashion statement. The tilaka, however, is a forehead mark worn by priests as a symbol of protection or to symbolize their connection to a certain god.

**Cows** are sacred symbols of fertility, charity, and love. Cows are worshipped with a puja.

**Astrologers** are often consulted to determine the best time for important events.

**Trees** are decorated with ribbons as an act of worship.

A **Sadhu** is a holy man who lives a life of self-denial. He may make great personal sacrifices—such as standing on one leg for a year.

**Vanaprastha** is the third stage of life, when a person partially retires from the world to focus on spiritual life.

The holy syllable **om**, which is in prayer and meditation.

ॐ

The god **Shiva** is associated with the power of destruction and transformation.

There are two teachings on breaking the cycle of reincarnation: the **way of the monkey** and the **way of the cat**. Those who follow the first teaching are freed by their own efforts, just as a baby monkey saves itself by actively hanging onto its mother for safety. Those who follow the second teaching trust in the saving power of a god, just as a baby cat lets itself be carried away by its mother.

Trees are sometimes dedicated to certain gods, and may be honored with a small **shrine** placed between the roots.

The **Vedas** are the oldest scriptures (a collection of sacred texts) of Hinduism.

**Hare Krishna** is a relatively young missionary movement that worships the god Krishna and seeks to spread his teachings throughout the world.

**Goats are sacrificed** in honor of certain fierce goddesses.

**Flower chains** symbolize gratitude and devotion.

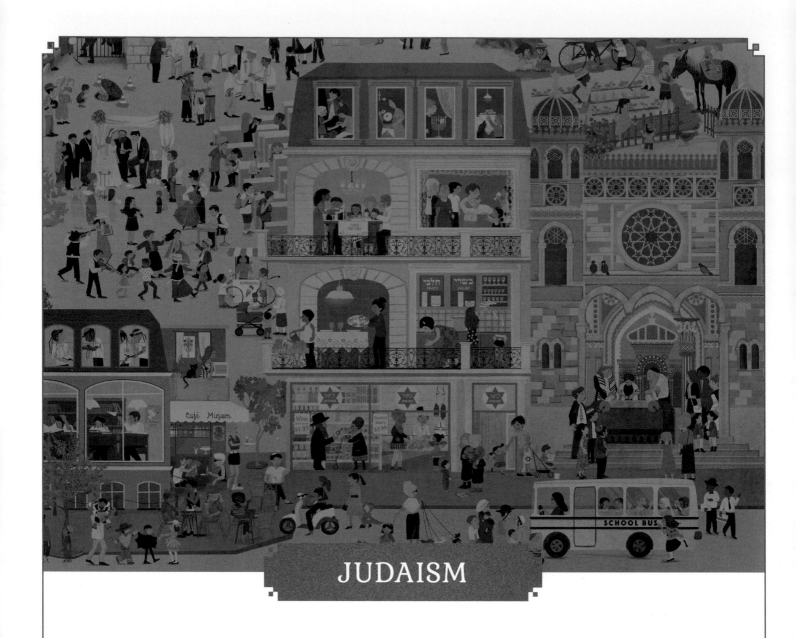

## JUDAISM

Judaism is the oldest religion to worship a single god. It is built upon the stories of Abraham and his descendants in the Hebrew bible. These same stories are also the foundation of Christianity and Islam. Although there are Jewish communities around the world, most Jews today live in Israel and the United States.

The holy book of Judaism is the Hebrew Bible, the Tanakh. It consists of three parts: the Torah (the five books of Moses), the Books of the Prophets, and a collection of further holy writings. A later work, the Talmud, outlines how to live a Jewish life.

If your mother is Jewish you are born into Judaism and automatically become a Jew as well. Judaism does not seek to convert others, but a person can convert after formal training.

In Judaism, God bears the Hebrew name YHVH, though out of respect the name is never spoken. Instead, he may be called Adonai (My Lord). At the heart of Judaism lies the agreement between God and the people of Israel. This agreement (called Brit in Hebrew) says that Adonai is the only god and the creator of the world, and that no other gods shall be worshipped before him. In exchange for their special relationship to him, the Jewish people work to follow God's laws.

According to the Tanakh, the prophet Moses received 613 laws from God, called commandments. These describe the agreement between God and the Jews, and instruct how the people should live and behave. God's commandments can be found in the Torah.

In Judaism, there is a belief in a Messiah who will come to bring a time of peace. But above all there is a strong focus on family, community, and living a good life with the help of the commandments.

The **Yochanan ben Zakai Synagogue** in Jerusalem was built in the early 1600s.

On the Temple Mount in Jerusalem stands the **Wailing Wall**, a holy site in Judaism. This western wall of the old Temple of Jerusalem is the only part that remains. Small notes with prayers, wishes, and thanks are tucked between the stones. Now and then, the notes are removed and buried on the Mount of Olives.

On the holiday of **Simchat Torah**, observed in autumn, the Torah is carried in a procession and joyously celebrated.

Also on **Temple Mount** stand the Al-Aqsa Mosque and the Dome of the Rock. Access to Temple Mount is strictly guarded, as it is the source of much conflict between Jews and Muslims, for whom it is also a holy site.

**Yom Kippur** is the day of atonement, when Jews confess their sins and seek forgiveness from each other as well as from God. It is the highest Jewish holiday and a strict day of prayer and fasting.

The **mezuzah** hangs on the right-hand side of a doorway, to be touched on entering and leaving. Inside it is a rolled-up parchment with a passage from the Torah. It is a sign of God's blessing and protection.

Jewish **marriage** vows traditionally take place under a canopy (chuppah). An important feature is the marriage contract (ketubbah). During the ceremony the bride and groom drink wine from a common cup, and the bridegroom then steps on a glass to smash it.

A traditional Jewish funeral includes a **burial**. It is customary to place a small bag containing soil from Israel in the coffin. To show their grief, the mourners rip their clothing.

**Tzitzis** are the four knotted fringes decorating the corners of the prayer shawl (tallit). When a tallit katan is worn beneath the clothing, the fringes show below the shirt.

**The Holocaust Memorial** in Berlin, Germany, was built to remember the Jews murdered in Europe during the Nazi regime. In Hebrew the Holocaust is called the Shoah, meaning a great catastrophe.

In the **Jewish calendar** the months are based on the lunar cycle, and the years on the revolution of Earth around the Sun.

**Kabbalah** is a form of Jewish mysticism focused on the secrets of the Torah.

The **menorah** is a seven-branched candelabra, a symbol of the Second Jerusalem Temple. It serves as a symbol of Judaism, but is no longer lit.

**Havdalah** means separation or difference. Braided Havdalah candles are lit at the end of most holidays to mark the separation between the holy and the everyday.

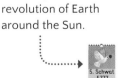

A **yeshivah** is a Jewish high school where mostly male students study the Torah and the Talmud. The Torah contains the five books of Moses. In the Talmud, questions about Jewish religious life are discussed.

**KIPPOT**

A **kippah, or yarmulken,** is a head covering worn by men, but also routinely by women, when they read the Torah or visit a synagogue or cemetery.

A **mikvah** is a bath used for ritual cleansing. Women visit the mikvah especially after menstruation or after childbirth. Men use it before holidays.

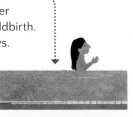

**Purim** is a feast that commemorates Queen Esther's rescue of the Jews in Persia two thousand years ago. Children dress up for this joyful celebration and eat sweets.

People ring in the Jewish New Year, called **Rosh Hashanah**, by blowing a ram's horn, or shofar. To ensure a sweet new year, they might eat apples with honey.

◀ The **prayer shawl, or tallit** is worn over the head and shoulders during prayer. It is sometimes worn for the first time at a child's bar or bat mitzvah.

**Sukkoth**, the Feast of the Tabernacles, was originally a harvest thanksgiving festival. Each year people build huts for the festival, in which they eat, celebrate, and sometimes sleep. The huts are a reminder of the temporary shelters that the Israelites lived in when they fled Egypt.

**Tefillin** are black leather boxes and leather straps. The boxes contain small parchment scrolls with texts from the Torah. The straps are wound around the head and left arm during morning prayers on weekdays.

**Sufganiyot** are doughnuts fried in oil and eaten for Hanukkah.

◀ The **Central Synagogue** is in New York City.

The **dreidel** is a four-sided top decorated with Hebrew letters. Children play with it on Hanukkah.

**Hanukkah** is the Jewish Festival of Lights, celebrated in November or December. The holiday lasts for eight days. Each evening an additional candle is lit in a special nine-branched menorah called a hanukkiah.

Boys are circumcised eight days after birth. The ceremony is called **brit mila or bris**, and is a symbol of the agreement between God and the Jewish people.

◀ The **Sabbath** is the day of rest in the Jewish week. It begins Friday evening with the lighting of two candles, a meal, and a worship service. The Sabbath ends at sundown on Saturday.

◀ A rule of Jewish food preparation says that **dairy and meat** must be cooked separately and never eaten together. This is why different cooking pots and dishes are used.

In the synagogue, services are attended by **rabbis** who guide worshippers in religious laws and spiritual care. Women rabbis can mostly be found in liberal congregations.

During **Passover**, Jews remember the liberation of the Israelites from slavery in Egypt. Friends and family gather for the evening seder and eat unleavened bread (matzoh), as the Israelites did. Before the holiday, all cooking pots and dishes are ritually cleaned to make sure they are free from traces of bread.

Jewish **dietary laws,** called kashrut, determine which foods are kosher (fit to eat) and which are not. For example, meat from cows and goats may be eaten, but meat from pigs and rabbits may not.

The **Star of David** is a symbol of Judaism and the people of Israel. ▶

A **Sefer Torah** is handwritten in Hebrew on a long roll of parchment. It is kept in a cabinet in the synagogue.

At a **bat mitzvah** (when girls reach age twelve) or bar mitzvah (when boys reach thirteen), children read from the Torah for the first time. They have reached their religious maturity and from this point are expected to follow all religious rules.

Jewish children attend both regular school and **Hebrew school** where they learn about their religion and the Hebrew language. ▶

## BUDDHISM

Buddhism is the fourth-largest religion in the world. It grew out of the Hindu traditions in India and became its own religion. Today most Buddhists live in Central, South, and Southeast Asia, and still others live in Europe, North America, and Australia.

Buddhism today is mainly based on two traditions—the Theravada (mostly practiced in Sri Lanka, Cambodia, Thailand, Laos, and Myanmar) and the Mahayana (most popular in Tibet, China, Taiwan, Japan, Vietnam, Korea, and Mongolia). There are many different smaller schools of thought as well.

In Buddhism, there is no creator god as there is, for example, in Hinduism and Judaism. Buddhism was founded by Siddhartha Gautama (sixth to fourth Century BCE). He was born a prince and decided to live his life without luxuries so he could concentrate fully on overcoming suffering. He realized in his search that living a balanced life (the middle way) led to happiness and release from suffering. Siddhartha Gautama became the first to bear the title Buddha, meaning the Enlightened One. He began to spread his teachings (dharma) in northern India.

Buddhists believe in reincarnation. Their highest goal is to be released, and to help others be released, from this eternal cycle of life, death, and rebirth, because in Buddhism, an unenlightened life necessarily includes suffering.

The basis of the Buddha's teachings are the Four Noble Truths. The first teaches that suffering is a part of life. The second teaches that the origin of suffering lies in selfish desires and cravings. The third teaches that an end to suffering is possible. The fourth teaches that to reach this state, you must follow the Noble Eightfold Path. The path is a guide to attitude, conduct, and meditation, and leads to the deliverance from suffering.

The White
Elephant

Learn to
Meditate

# BUDDHISM

The **Boudhanath Stupa** is a shrine in Kathmandu, Nepal. Buddhists circle the shrine clockwise to show their deep respect to the site.

In Tibet, the custom of **sky burials** is widespread. The dead are kept at home for several days as prayers guide their spirit toward a good rebirth. The body is then taken to a sacred burial site and left to the elements. This ritual is considered an act of generosity, because the body feeds other living creatures.

◀ A Tibetan **prayer wheel** contains small rolls of paper with mantras, or holy words or syllables, written on them. On each turn of the wheel a mantra is recited and carried out into the world.

◀ The **eternal knot** is one of the Eight Sacred Symbols, called Ashtamangala. It symbolizes the eternity of Buddha's wisdom and compassion.

◀ Monks are highly respected in Buddhism. To receive a blessing from a monk, you can offer **food donations**.

**Daibutsu**, a statue of the Great Buddha, stands on the grounds of the Kotoku-in temple in Kamakura, Japan.

In Buddhist countries, anyone can attend **open-air lectures** to learn about Buddhist teachings. ▶

**Obon** is a Japanese festival that honors the spirits of people's ancestors. Family members come together for celebration and dancing. Lanterns guide the ancestral spirits back to the world of the dead.

**Wat Arun**, the Temple of Dawn, stands in Bangkok, Thailand.

In Japan, flower arrangement is called **Ikebana**. This spiritual art form is a way to develop sensitivity, mindfulness, and attention.

TIbetan pilgrims leave **mani stones** on the path to or in front of temples. They are often inscribed with the mantra, "om mani padme hum."

**Tibetan cham dances** are usually led by monks wearing masks to represent various gods. Elements of the dances come from the Bon religion, an older tradition from Tibet.

In Buddhism, a string of prayer beads is called a **mala**. It is often made of 108 small beads and one large one.

The **Dharma Wheel** (dharmachakra) is a symbol of Buddhism. The eight ▶ spokes stand for the Noble Eightfold Path, which will free you from the eternal cycle of rebirth.

Buddha Day, also called **Vesak Day**, is a reminder of the birth of Buddha, his enlightenment, and his death—when he left the cycle of reincarnation. Usually celebrated in late spring/early summer, it is the most sacred Buddhist holiday.

**Meditation** improves mindfulness and concentration. There are many different ways to mediate. Often ▶ mantras are spoken. In Buddhism, meditation is considered part of the way to enlightenment.

◀······ In Buddhism, the **dragon** possesses special powers and stands for rebirth, change, and renewal. It is often part of Buddha Day.

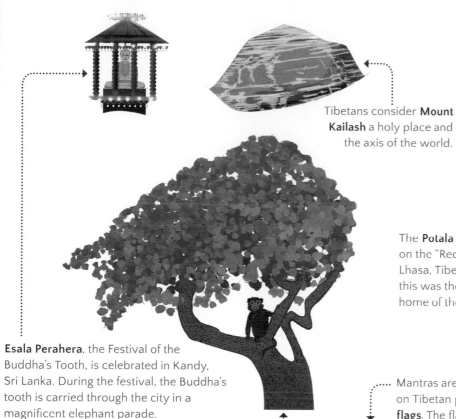

Tibetans consider **Mount Kailash** a holy place and the axis of the world.

**Enso**, or the Sign of the Circle, is a symbol of emptiness. It is drawn by people in a meditative state.

The **Potala Palace** sits on the "Red Hill" in Lhasa, Tibet. Until 1959, this was the winter home of the Dalai Lama.

The writing of characters and pictures is called **calligraphy**. In Buddhism it is a tool to practice mindfulness.

**Esala Perahera**, the Festival of the Buddha's Tooth, is celebrated in Kandy, Sri Lanka. During the festival, the Buddha's tooth is carried through the city in a magnificent elephant parade.

The Bodhi Tree grows at the **Mahabodhi Temple** in Bodh Gaya in India. It was here that the Buddha was enlightened, and it remains a destination for Buddhist pilgrims.

In Japan, the Buddha's birthday is called **Kanbutsu-e**. It's celebrated April 8.

Mantras are written on Tibetan **prayer flags**. The flags flutter in the wind, which sends the prayers out in all directions.

The **lotus blossom** is one of the Eight Sacred Symbols. It stands for purity and enlightenment.

The **Way of the Tea** is a ceremony in which the host and the guest prepare and drink tea together. Each step of the ritual is carried out with attention and care.

The **two golden fish** are one of the Eight Sacred Symbols. The fish represent fearlessness.

Buddhist **weddings** do not follow any specific format. In one custom from Thailand, guests pour water over the hands of the bridal couple, symbolizing purification and a new beginning.

The **Bongeunsa Temple**, which means "Offering Support," is in Seoul, South Korea.

After the birth of a child, a monk advises on the choice of a name. A **fire ritual** is said to protect the newborn from evil influences and bring good life energy.

The **Buddhist flag** has been recognized as the international symbol of Buddhism since 1950.

In Thailand, Songkran is celebrated April 13 to 15. These **New Year's** festivities are particularly exuberant. According to custom, statues of the Buddha are bathed with water, which can lead to real water fights.

Children, women and young men can enter a monastery for a time to study Buddhism. They **shave their hair** beforehand to emphasize similarity with the monks and nuns, and to show that they have turned away from all worldly concerns and dedicated themselves to religion.

There is no holy text in Buddhism, but there are many sacred writings, called canons. Among the oldest canons is the **Pali Canon**, or Tripitaka ("three baskets").

**Mandalas** are complex symbols made by monks and used as concentration exercises. When the shapes are drawn with sand, they are destroyed when finished, as a reminder of impermanence (meaning nothing lasts forever).

## CHRISTIANITY

Christianity has more followers than any other world religion. It grew out of Judaism about two thousand years ago. Christianity consists of several different denominations and groups. The three largest are Catholicism, Eastern Orthodoxy, and Protestantism.

Christians believe in a single god as the creator of the world and of life. God is seen as the source of love and faith. They also believe that God is made up of three persons—the Father, the Son, and the Holy Spirit—called the Trinity.

Jesus is considered the son of God. He is referred to as Christ, which means savior or Messiah. His teachings speak of unconditional love toward humans and God. Jesus had many followers, called disciples, and these people said that he performed miracles and above all helped outcasts and the needy. But there were also those who rejected him, because he criticized their behavior and actions.

Jesus Christ was crucified, or put to death on the cross, by the Romans. The cross is a symbol of his self-sacrifice. According to tradition, after his death, Jesus rose from the dead and ascended into heaven to God. Christians see Jesus's life, death, and resurrection as an example of how humans can be saved from a life of sin. The belief in life after death—whether one goes to heaven or hell—is central to Christian belief.

You can read about the life and teachings of Jesus in the New Testament, which is the second part of the Christian Bible, the holy book of Christians. The first part is referred to as the Old Testament, which includes stories about, among other things, the Ten Commandments that God revealed to Moses.

The **Church of the Holy Sepulchre** is in Jerusalem. This is where Jesus is said to have been crucified, ▶ buried, and resurrected.

**Gospel** means "good news." It also describes the church music of the African American community.

◀ Monks and nuns often live in **monasteries or convents**, where they devote their lives to their religion.

Traditionally, after the **funeral ceremony** the deceased is buried. Often a gravestone is erected in his or her memory.

**Missionary work** is aimed at converting people to the Christian faith. In some countries, missionaries perform aid and development work. ▶

A pilgrimage is a journey to a holy place. During ▶ pilgrimages the faithful seek to become closer to God and atone for their sins.

**Mennonites** belong to an offshoot of the Protestant tradition. They strive to live a communal life similar to that of the early Christians.

The **Day of the Dead** is one of the most ▶ important festivals in Mexico. It coincides with All Saints' Day (November 1) and All Souls' Day (November 2).

The **Copts** are members of the largest Christian Church in Egypt. Monastery life and social work play a central role in their faith. As in the Catholic Church, the head of the Church is called a pope.

**Pentecostalism** is a relatively recent movement of Christianity that emphasizes a personal experience of God. Pentecostal gatherings are often enthusiastic and emotional, and are sometimes broadcast by TV, radio, and online.

The **Via Dolorosa** means "the painful path." A famous Christian holy site in Jerusalem, it's believed to be the route Jesus walked to his crucifixion.

**St. Peter's** in Rome, Italy, is the largest basilica in the world. It stands on the spot where St. Peter the Apostle is believed to be buried.

The sign of the **fish** is a very old symbol of Christianity. The Greek word for "fish," *icthys*, is an anagram for the Greek words meaning "Jesus Christ, Son of God and Savior."

**Holy Thursday**, celebrated in the spring, remembers the Last Supper, which Jesus shared with his disciples.

The **Bible** is the holy book of Christianity and is made up of the Old and New Testaments.

The **Virgin Mary** is particularly revered in the Catholic and Orthodox faiths as the mother of Jesus Christ. She is honored with prayers, pilgrimages, and festivals.

The **Eucharist**, also called Holy Communion, is usually celebrated on Sundays. In this ritual, Christians receive bread and wine as a reminder of Jesus's sacrifice. Here, the Eucharist is being celebrated at **Holy Mass on Easter**.

The **dove** symbolizes the Holy Spirit. ▶

Through **baptism** the faithful are cleansed of their sins and ▶ brought into the church community.

Every Catholic church has a **confessional**, where believers come to admit their sins and make things right with God.

**Incense** is the fragrant resin of the frankincense tree. It is burned during certain rituals of Catholic and Eastern Orthodox Churches. It represents purification and devotion.

Catholics cross themselves with **holy water** from a basin at the entrance to their church as a reminder of baptism.

**St. Martin's Day** (November 11) commemorates St. Martin of Tours, a Roman soldier who gave a beggar half of his cloak.

The **Luther rose** is a symbol of the Lutheran Church. The cross inside the heart represents belief in the crucified Jesus Christ.

The **Ethiopian Church** is the largest of the Oriental Orthodox Churches.

**Easter**, the most important event in the Christian year, celebrates the resurrection of Christ. In northern European countries, a bonfire is lit the evening before Easter Sunday.

The **Baptist Church** is an offshoot of the Protestant tradition. Baptists decide as adults whether to recognize the faith and are then baptized into it.

The **Advent calendar** and the **Advent wreath** are traditions of Advent, which marks the beginning of the Christmas season.

**C + M + B** stands for "Christus mansionem benedicat" (Latin for Christ bless this house). It also represents the first letters of the names of the Three Wise Men: Caspar, Melchior, and Balthazar.

In many countries, a tree is put up and decorated at **Christmas**, though no one knows exactly where this custom came from.

20*C+M+B+17

The birth of Jesus is celebrated on Christmas. The **manger** symbolizes his birth in a stable.

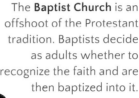

The **cross** is a symbol of Christianity, since Jesus died on a cross.

The **Cathedral of Christ the Savior** in Moscow is the main church of the Russian Orthodox Church.

**Jehovah's Witnesses** believe that the world can be divided into good and evil, and that the end is near. They reject many of the teachings of traditional Christian Churches and actively try to convert other people to their faith.

On January 6, children in the Czech Republic dress up as the Three Wise Men, also called the **Three Kings**, who were said to have brought gifts to Jesus after his birth. They collect donations for charity and write good wishes on houses.

In many European countries, children place their shoes outside the door on the night before **St. Nicholas Day** (December 6), in hopes that they will be filled with gifts by morning.

A procession is a both a celebration and a religious ritual. Catholics in Spain wear hooded robes to take part in **Passion processions**. These robes come from a medieval tradition. The parades reenact the events leading to Jesus's crucifixion.

Believers of the Eastern Orthodox Church use pictures called **icons** to worship Christ and the saints.

The **rosary** is a prayer necklace. It usually consists of 59 beads, with each one representing a prayer.

**Communion** is an admission ritual in the Catholic Church. Before being admitted to the church, children are instructed in Christian beliefs.

◀ As part of the **marriage ceremony in the Orthodox Church** the bride and groom will drink from a single cup, circle the altar three times, and have their hands bound together. These rituals represent their commitment to each other and the connection between Christ and the Church.

**Charity** is central to the mission of many Christian organizations and independent churches. They encourage social work and support for the needy.

The **pope** is the head of the Catholic Church. He is sometimes driven around in a special car called the popemobile.

## ISLAM

Islam is the youngest of the five major world religions. It is called an Abrahamic religion because it recognizes Abraham, a figure in the Bible, as the first prophet. Like Jews and Christians, followers of Islam, called Muslims, believe in a single god as the creator of the world. They call him Allah.

Muslims make up the second-largest religious community after Christians. Anyone who has a Muslim parent or makes a confession of faith before two witnesses is a Muslim. In Islam, there is no central authority. Each community appoints a prayer leader, called an imam. After a political conflict in the seventh century, there emerged two branches of Islam, Sunni and Shiite.

Islam developed in Mecca, in what is now Saudi Arabia. That's where Muhammad was born in 570. According to Islam, he is the last in a series of prophets that includes Abraham, Moses, and Jesus. Muslims believe that the angel Gabriel revealed to Muhammad the text of the Islamic holy book, called the Qu'ran. The Qu'ran is the sacred word of Allah. From this, as well as the traditions and declarations of the prophet, come all the moral rules and rituals of Islam.

At the heart of Islam are the Five Pillars. These are the five basic acts all Muslims must complete if they want to live a good and moral life. They are Shahada (declaring your faith), Salat (reciting the five daily prayers), Zakat (donating alms, or money, to the needy), Sawm (fasting during the month of Ramadan), and Hajj (making a pilgrimage to Mecca). Muslims also believe in the Last Judgment, which means that after death, people are judged for their deeds and the depth of their faith. Those who have lived good lives will go to paradise, while those who have not will go to hell.

# ISLAM

The **Great Mosque of Djenné** in Mali is built of clay.

The **muezzin** calls people to prayer five times each day.

For Shiites, **Ashura** commemorates the death of Imam Hussein. He was the son of Ali, the first leader of Shiite Muslims.

The hands, arms, and feet of Muslim brides are often decorated with **henna** the evening before the wedding.

In many mosques, you will find a **madrassa**, a school where Islam is taught.

The **Tuaregs** traditionally lived as nomads moving from place to place in the desert. Because of this they played an important role in the spread of Islam in North Africa.

In Islam, the **dead** are traditionally wrapped in linen cloth. They are buried lying on their right side, facing the direction of Mecca. It is uncommon for women to accompany the funeral procession to the cemetery.

A child is given a name no more than one week after **birth**. The child's hair is shaved and weighed. The weight in gold or silver is given to charity.

The **Minangkabau** people are indigenous to the Indonesian island of Sumatra. Although they are Muslims, they also have a culture that believes in female succession.

**Sufism** is a branch of Islam that seeks closeness to God through repetitive rituals and devotional acts called dhikr. Some forms of dhikr resemble dancing.

Giving **alms**, such as money or food to those in need, is a core duty of every Muslim.

The **Ka'ba** is described as the "house of God." This large cube structure, draped with fabric, stands in the courtyard of the Great Mosque of Mecca. Pilgrims circle the Ka'ba during the Hajj.

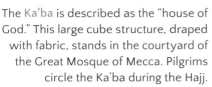

**Calligraphy** is an important Islamic art form.

The **Hand of Fatima** is a sign of blessing and good luck.

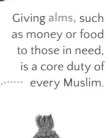

The **Shahada** is the declaration of faith in Islam: "I proclaim that there is no God but Allah, and that Muhammad is his messenger."

Many Muslims celebrate Muhammad's birthday on **Mawlid an-Nabi**. They decorate their homes and take part in large processions, or parades, like this one in Indonesia.

The double-bladed sword, **Zulfiqar**, is often used as a symbol of the Shiites.

Muslims, like Jewish boys, are **circumcised**.

According to Islam, a man can have up to four wives (**polygamy**), as long as it is legally allowed and he can provide for all his family members. But the actual practice of polygamy is very uncommon.

Muslims need a clean surface on which to pray. This is the reason for a **prayer carpet**, which must be used with clean feet and no shoes.

At the end of the Islamic year, there is a large **pilgrimage** (Hajj), or journey, to Mecca. Every Muslim must try to make this pilgrimage at least once in his or her life. In Egypt, the homes of the pilgrims are often decorated and painted.

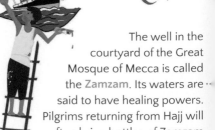

The well in the courtyard of the Great Mosque of Mecca is called the **Zamzam**. Its waters are said to have healing powers. Pilgrims returning from Hajj will often bring bottles of Zamzam water to friends and family.

The **Qu'ran** is the holy book of Islam. It consists of 114 surahs, or chapters.

Muslims fast during the month of Ramadan, eating and drinking nothing between sunrise and sunset. In Turkey and other Muslim countries, drummers wake the faithful for the pre-dawn meal, Suhoor.

The Fatima Masuma Mosque in Qom, Iran, is an important site for Shiites.

Eid al-Fitr is a three-day festival marking the end of the fasting month of Ramadan.

The shrine to Fatima Masuma, on the site of the mosque also named for her, is a popular pilgrimage destination.

Before a wedding, a contract is made between the two families to determine the amount of the gift (mehr) that the bridegroom promises to pay to the bride.

The Al-Aqsa Mosque in Jerusalem stands near a shrine called the Dome of the Rock. The rock inside is sacred to Muslims and Jews, and is often the source of conflict. Also nearby is the gravesite of Jesus, in the Church of the Holy Sepulchre.

The Basmala is a phrase that is recited before each chapter of the Qu'ran is read: "In the name of God, the most Gracious and most Merciful."

An imam is a person who leads a group in prayer. If a group includes only women and children, a woman may lead the prayer, but she is forbidden to do this if grown men are present.

Alcohol and pork are considered haram, or forbidden. Muslims must only eat meat from animals that have been killed according to ritual procedures called halal.

Five times a day, Muslims face Mecca and pray. Men and women are mostly separated during prayer.

The Islamic calendar is a lunar calendar with twelve months.

Indonesia is the country with the largest number of Muslims.

Before prayers, Muslims must perform a ritual washing. Each mosque includes a place for washing—often a fountain or well.

Hilal is the Arabic word for "crescent." This symbolizes the new moon, which begins each month in the Islamic calendar.

All women must wear head scarves during prayer and when visiting a mosque.

The four-day festival of Eid al-Adha, the Feast of the Sacrifice, honors the prophet Abraham. Traditionally, an animal is sacrificed at this celebration, with a third of the meat given to neighbors and a third to the poor.

The misbaha is a string of prayer beads. There are usually ninety-nine beads, as a reminder of the ninety-nine names of Allah.